I0878921

Spotlight on Social Justice

TO ARM OR DISARM?

ADDRESSING GUN VIOLENCE

DENISE CLAY-MURRAY

TFCB

TWENTY-FIRST CENTURY BOOKS / MINNEAPOLIS

For Phelan, Sherrie, Sheena, Keisha, Solisha, Jack, and Sharon, my nieces and nephews who were allowed, for the most part, to be kids.

Copyright © 2025 by Lerner Publishing Group, Inc.

All rights reserved. International copyright secured. No part of this book may be reproduced, stored in a retrieval system, or transmitted in any form or by any means—electronic, mechanical, photocopying, recording, or otherwise—without the prior written permission of Lerner Publishing Group, Inc., except for the inclusion of brief quotations in an acknowledged review.

Twenty-First Century Books™
An imprint of Lerner Publishing Group, Inc.
241 First Avenue North
Minneapolis, MN 55401 USA

For reading levels and more information, look up this title at www.lernerbooks.com.

Main body text set in Bembo Std Regular
Typeface provided by Monotype Typography.

Library of Congress Cataloging-in-Publication Data

Names: Clay-Murray, Denise, author.
Title: To arm or disarm? : addressing gun violence / Denise Clay-Murray.
Description: Minneapolis : Twenty-First Century Books, [2025] | Series: Spotlight on social justice | Includes bibliographical references and index. | Audience: Ages 11–18 | Audience: Grades 7–9 | Summary: "North American civilians own more than 400 million guns, and more than half of US adults know someone who has been a victim of gun violence. Explore what gun violence is, what influences it, the debate over gun control measures, and more"— Provided by publisher.
Identifiers: LCCN 2024010768 (print) | LCCN 2024010769 (ebook) | ISBN 9798765627211 (library binding) | ISBN 9798765662595 (paperback) | ISBN 9798765659540 (epub)
Subjects: LCSH: Gun control—United States—Juvenile literature. | Violent crimes—United States—Juvenile literature. | Firearms—United States—Juvenile literature.
Classification: LCC HV7436 .C53 2025 (print) | LCC HV7436 (ebook) | DDC 363.330973—dc23/eng/20240416

LC record available at https://lccn.loc.gov/2024010768
LC ebook record available at https://lccn.loc.gov/2024010769

Manufactured in the United States of America
2-1014155-52103-3/24/2026

CONTENTS

INTRODUCTION

During Philadelphia's 2023 Democratic primary for mayor, city councilmember Kenyatta Johnson held a discussion focused on gun violence. Seven of the eleven people running for mayor attended. The mayoral candidates shared their visions of how they'd help gun violence victims and co-victims—people who are affected by but not the direct targets of gun violence—with the audience.

The discussion ran smoothly until a staffer from Johnson's office brought a small girl to the stage. The girl, who was about five years old, had lost her father to gun violence when she was two. She wanted to know what the candidates would do to make sure that what happened to her didn't happen to other children. The audience, the candidates, and even the event's moderator tried to keep their composure as the child's tears flowed. That someone so young had already lost a parent to gun violence highlighted the reality of the problem in the United States.

But what is gun violence? It includes violent crimes such as mass shootings and homicide. It also includes accidental death or injury, and suicide. According to a study from Everytown for Gun Safety, an organization that focuses

In 2023 people joined a Silence the Violence march in Detroit, Michigan. They held posters of victims of gun violence. They were protesting the almost-daily shootings in the city, which killed more than 760 young people that year.

on preventing gun violence, 59 percent of all adults in the US know someone who has been a victim of gun violence, including 71 percent of Black adults, 60 percent of Latine adults, and 58 percent of white adults.

The numbers are not much better for children and young adults. In their 2021 report, the Children's Defense Fund called gun violence the number one cause of death for people between the ages of one and nineteen. In 2020 the gun death rate among this age group in the US was 5 for every 100,000 youth, as opposed to Canada, which had a rate of 0.6 deaths for every 100,000 youth.

Organizations throughout North America are trying to curb gun violence. But, particularly in the US, not everyone agrees on the best or right way to do that.

Owning a Gun

The US has the highest rate of gun ownership in the world. In 2023, 61 percent of Americans said they believed guns were too easy to get. Many Americans believed that gun violence was a nationwide problem (75 percent) and that it was going to get worse over the next five years (62 percent).

Other North American countries have fewer guns and different restrictions. Canada has the seventh highest rate of gun ownership in the world, with 22 percent of Canadians owning a gun. Canada has stricter gun laws than the US, but Canadians are allowed to own firearms if they have a license.

Mexico is ranked fifty-third in gun ownership worldwide. Mexico has stricter gun laws than the US and Canada. Individuals go through months of background checks. They must show a birth certificate and proof that they are employed and have no criminal record. Having to go through so much paperwork, as well as there being only one gun store in the country, has encouraged some people in Mexico to smuggle in guns from the US. In 2023 more than 500 thousand guns were smuggled into Mexico from the US, and 70 percent of guns recovered from crime scenes in Mexico can be traced back to the US.

Mexico's only gun store is in Mexico City, and the government owns it. Customers must give authorities their cellphones, remove their hats, and pass through a metal detector before shopping.

In 2008 the Mexican army seized a record 540 weapons from a criminal organization. Most of the weapons could be traced to the US.

Gun Control

The US has a complex relationship with guns. Around the world, most countries have strict gun control laws that prevent or restrict their use. But in the US, gun regulation continues to be a political issue. While some politicians and citizens support strict gun control, others fall somewhere in the middle of total control and no control. Still others believe that the right to bear arms is sacred.

Many gun owners say owning a gun is connected to their personal freedom. But many critics of gun ownership say that personal freedom is nurtured at the expense of public safety. Regardless of whether they support gun control, many people, particularly in the US, have been put into a position where simple activities such as going to the corner store, attending a concert, or even walking to their math class can put them in the line of gunfire and change their lives forever.

While you might see instances of gun violence reported on the nightly news, what's reported is not the entire story. And knowing the entire story is important. This book will discuss the history of guns, why different communities may view guns differently, and what's being done at national and local levels to address gun violence. Gun violence can be difficult to talk about, especially if someone has experienced trauma from it. But understanding this issue, the different arguments surrounding it, and the people whom it has impacted is an important step in bringing about change.

Seventy-eight percent of US gun owners who grew up with guns in their households say that the right to own guns is about their personal freedom.

Studies have shown that California's strict gun laws have led to fewer incidents of gun violence in the state. In 2023 California governor Gavin Newsom (*center*) signed new gun control measures into law.

Gun Regulations in the US

There are some US federal regulations regarding guns, such as restricting the ownership of short-barreled shotguns, machine guns, and silencers. However, most gun policies are carried out at the state level. Some states have strict gun laws that regulate everything from who can have a gun to what kinds of guns are illegal to own, while other states have far fewer regulations.

For example, if you want to carry a concealed weapon in California, you're not only required to have a permit, but you must also have training. But to do the same in Florida, you need neither a permit nor training.

CHAPTER ONE

Nations at Gunpoint

The relationship between guns and North America goes back centuries. As European colonization and settlement began in the late 1400s, European explorers brought guns to North America, mainly for protection and hunting. Many historians think the Spanish were the first Europeans to bring guns to the Americas.

The Second Amendment

Gun use was widespread in the US during the Revolutionary War (1775–1783) between the US and Britain. Both British and American soldiers' main weapon was the musket gun. After winning the war, the US began shaping a new nation, leading to the writing of the Constitution in 1787. During this time, political discussions and debates centered around defining citizen's rights. The Second Amendment to the United States Constitution is part of the Bill of Rights and was adopted in 1791. It states: "A well-regulated Militia, being necessary to the security of a free State, the right of the people to keep and bear Arms, shall not be infringed."

Revolutionary War muskets weighed about 10 pounds (4.5 kg). Soldiers could fire three shots per minute on average.

This amendment came at a time when the newly independent country had no national military. Towns instead relied on local militias for protection. While the need for local militias slowly dissolved once the US Army National Guard was created in 1636, the need for protection is still at the center of most gun ownership. In 2023, 72 percent of all US gun owners cited protection as the reason they have a gun in their homes.

Gun rights supporters see ownership and access to guns as a constitutional right due to the Second Amendment. But those who advocate for gun control believe the amendment only applies to militias. Some gun control advocates also argue that the founding fathers had no idea how powerful and destructive guns would be in the future compared to guns in the 1700s.

The Gun Fighters

One of the strongest advocates for the rights of gun owners is the National Rifle Association (NRA). Colonel William Church and General George Wingate created the organization in 1871 with the goal of improving the marksmanship of US soldiers. The NRA has also organized gun competitions and created gun safety programs for youth and self-defense programs for women.

But the NRA has been most effective in its legislative efforts. The NRA's legislative arm, the Institute for Legislative Action, keeps its more than four million members up to date on the nation's gun laws. The Institute for Legislative Action also mobilizes NRA members to advocate against any law infringing on the right to own a firearm. Since the NRA's members are also consistent voters, legislators pay close attention to them. For example, thanks to the Institute for Legislative Action's efforts, people can legally carry a gun without applying for a permit in twenty-five US states.

On the other side of the gun debate is Everytown for Gun Safety. Everytown was formed in 2013 when two other groups, Moms Demand Action for Gun Sense in America and Mayors Against Illegal Guns, joined forces to advocate for what they consider common sense gun

The NRA holds an annual event for its members. The event showcases new gun technology and features seminars about gun rights issues.

In 2019 Everytown for Gun Safety activists in New Jersey supported governor Phil Murphy's (*center*) signing of an executive order to address gun violence.

legislation. They are the largest gun violence prevention organization in the US.

Like the NRA, Everytown organizes and encourages their members to contact their legislators and advocate for regulations such as mandatory background checks for gun purchasers. Through their efforts, several states have created gun violence prevention units, and many have passed laws keeping guns out of the hands of domestic abusers. Everytown also provides support for survivors of gun violence and researches the causes of gun violence.

REFLECT

Do you believe there should be stricter or looser laws on gun ownership? Why?

Rural vs. Urban Communities

The different environments people grow up in and their comfort level with guns can also shape their attitudes toward gun control and gun violence. There are more gun owners in US rural areas (47 percent) than there are in the suburbs (30 percent) and in urban areas (20 percent). Those in rural communities who own a gun often own more than one gun. People who live in rural communities are also more likely to have fired a gun than people who live in urban communities.

The difference between these two groups isn't unique to the United States. In Canada, people in rural communities

According to a federal study, about ten million Americans used firearms for hunting in 2016.

are also more likely to own a gun than their urban neighbors. Studies show that 37 percent of Canadians living in small towns own a gun, while that number goes down to 3 percent in communities with populations over one million.

Much of the difference in gun ownership by community is related to exposure to guns. While young people in rural communities are often exposed to guns earlier through hunting, skeet shooting, and other recreational activities involving firearms, this isn't necessarily the experience for young people in urban areas. Someone raised in a rural setting where guns are more often part of daily life may be more against strict gun control than someone from an urban environment where gun use isn't as common.

The perceived need for owning a gun can also differ in urban areas from rural ones. Urban areas often experience higher crime rates, and this can impact how people think about the need for guns in society. Urban gun owners often cite personal protection as their primary reason for owning a gun. On the other hand, supporters of gun control in urban areas may emphasize the need to reduce gun violence.

People in rural areas, who often experience less gun violence, might disagree more with gun control and focus instead on individual gun ownership rights. However, there are also gun control supporters in rural areas. Rural communities are seeing a rise in gun violence. From 2016 to 2020, the two US counties that experienced the most gun homicides per person were rural counties in Arkansas and Alabama. Some individuals in rural areas support gun control because they believe stricter regulations such as background checks

REFLECT

How do you think people's opinions about gun control and gun violence might be influenced by where they live or their personal experiences?

could help prevent gun violence, including mass shootings and incidents of domestic violence involving firearms.

People's reasons for supporting gun control or owning a gun can be complex. Many factors including personal experiences, perceptions of safety, cultural backgrounds, and political beliefs can influence those reasons. The urban and rural divide contributes to the ongoing gun control debate. Different perspectives and lived experiences lead to strong positions on both sides. But one thing is for certain—there are many guns and many ideas, arguments, and opinions about them in North America.

From 2016 to 2020, Phillips County in Arkansas had the most gun homicides per person in the US.

How Many Guns?

A 2017 survey in Canada shows that Canadian civilians own about 12.7 million guns. According to a 2022 report, there were 17 million guns in civilian hands in Mexico and 393 million guns in civilian hands in the United States.

If that sounds like a lot, that's because it is. The population of the US was just over 340 million in 2023. That means the US had more guns than people. The country that is closest to the US in terms of civilian gun possession is India, which has more than 71 million guns in civilian hands. But its population is much higher at 1.43 billion people.

Vijayawada is one of India's oldest cities. In India, gun laws are strict, and gun ownership is rare. According to the 2019 Small Arms Survey, India ranks 110th globally in civilian firearm ownership with 4.2 guns per one hundred people. In comparison, the US ranks first with 120.5 guns per one hundred people.

CHAPTER TWO

Gun Violence and Disinvestment

Many social scientists agree that gun violence is connected to disinvestment, also known as structural inequality. While investment means putting money or other resources into a person, place, or thing, disinvestment means the opposite—not putting money or other resources into a person, place, or thing, even when it's needed.

Structural inequality is often based on race and class. Most forms of disinvestment are concentrated in Black and Brown neighborhoods. Disinvestment, like investment, takes a lot of forms. If a school doesn't have enough books or the books are outdated, that's a form of disinvestment. If the only thing resembling a grocery store in someone's neighborhood is a corner store where products are expensive and healthful food is in short supply, that's a form of disinvestment. And if there are many people who either don't have jobs or have jobs that barely cover expenses including rent, food, heat, and Internet access, that's a form of disinvestment.

REFLECT

How might disinvestment impact individuals, families, and businesses within a community?

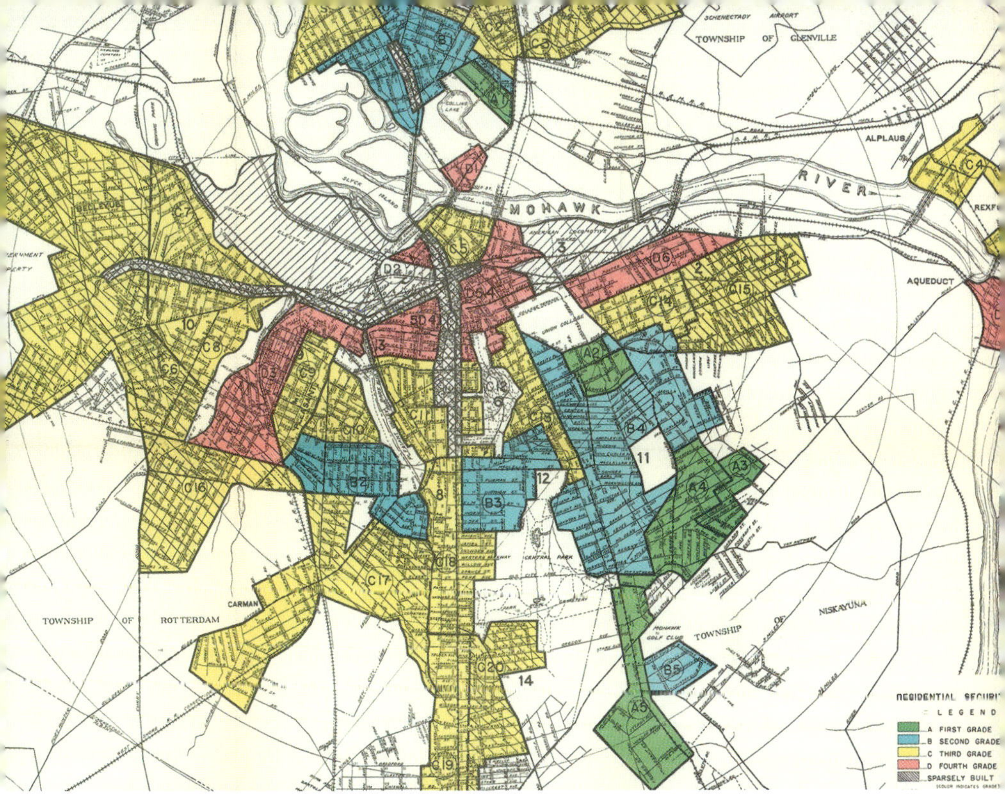

A Federal Home Loan Bank Board map of Schenectady, New York, from the 1930s. The map's red areas are largely Black communities. Residents who lived in these areas were denied home loans.

Redlining

Many studies show that redlining is one of the forms of disinvestment that has contributed most to gun violence. Redlining is when lending institutions such as banks and credit unions draw a "red line" around certain neighborhoods. Lending institutions decide that lending money to people in these neighborhoods is a financial risk, no matter what their credit score—a number predicting how likely a person is to pay back a loan on time—is. This makes it hard for the people in these neighborhoods to get loans to start businesses or buy homes despite being otherwise qualified.

Though redlining became illegal in 1968, many studies show that its effects continue. And discrimination in lending institutions still exists. One study in 2020 showed that most Black families who own a home in a neighborhood that was redlined have lost at least $212,000 in personal wealth over the last forty years.

The poverty that redlining has helped create is associated with increased rates of gun violence. Research also shows that Black and Brown people whose homes were redlined into low-income neighborhoods with few resources and opportunities experience more hopelessness and higher rates of gun violence. And higher rates of gun violence make this feeling of hopelessness even worse, which creates even more gun violence.

Research also shows that gun violence may be concentrated in some neighborhoods because violence causes more violence. People who are victims of violence are 3.5 times more likely to commit violence themselves.

Gun Violence Is a Racial Justice Issue

From 2019 through 2022, the US cities that had the highest gun homicide rates were Detroit, Memphis, and St. Louis. Other cities with high gun homicide rates include Philadelphia, New Orleans, and Baltimore. What these cities have in common are large, often segregated, Black communities with a history of disinvestment and redlining.

Black US citizens are two times more likely than white US citizens to die from gun violence. They are fourteen times more likely to be wounded by a gun and ten times more likely to die from gun homicide. Gun homicide among all Hispanic people is also more than double the non-Hispanic white gun homicide rate. Thirty-four Black people and

Arizona has the highest rate of Latine gun violence death in the US. A 2018 march protesting gun violence in Arizona drew more than fifteen thousand people.

thirteen Latine people are killed with guns every day. Also, one in three Black or Latine people know someone who was killed with a gun. Black and Latine men in disinvested communities make up most gun homicides in cities.

Gun violence statistics by race are not much better in Canada. Black neighborhoods in Toronto have more incidences of gun violence, especially homicides. And these neighborhoods have experienced a steady increase in gun violence between 2013 and 2022 that seems likely to continue.

Fixing disinvestment takes effort, money, and political will. Some nonprofit organizations are putting in the effort and using the money they've raised to help. They are creating training and economic development programs that are making a difference.

Both racial justice and efforts to end gun violence strive for equality. Racial justice aims to address inequality and discrimination that affect communities. Similarly, campaigns against gun violence seek to ensure that all individuals, regardless of race, are able to live in safe communities free from the threat of gun violence.

YouthBuild Philly

As part of the 2021 budget, Philadelphia created the Community Expansion Grant program. To receive a grant, an organization had to have a track record working with areas most impacted by gun violence. Preference was given to organizations serving Black and Brown men and boys between the ages of sixteen and thirty-four because that is the population most impacted by gun violence in the city. YouthBuild Philly is one of thirty-one entities that received money through the Expansion Grant Program.

"YouthBuild sits at the epicenter of all of the different things that we are seeing as issues in communities that marginalized groups live in," said Le'Yondo Dunn, YouthBuild Philly's CEO. "There are neighborhoods where you cannot find access to fresh and healthy foods because grocery stores don't exist. There are neighborhoods that have high populations of folks who have not completed a high school diploma. There are neighborhoods where there are high rates of drug crime. There are neighborhoods that have high rates of violent crime.

Students from YouthBuild Philly work on a gutted rowhouse. The two-year program offers young adults a high school diploma while developing vital job skills through academics, vocational training, and community service.

Our students primarily come to us from those areas. And we know that when young people are disengaged, and they're disconnected from school, they are more likely to either be perpetrators or victims of gun violence."

An evaluation of the program that the Philadelphia-based organization Equal Measure conducted showed that most of the program's grants are reaching Black and Latine men between the ages of sixteen and thirty-four. These grant efforts are showing positive results. As of 2023 homicides in Philadelphia were down 26 percent, and shootings overall were down 22 percent since 2021.

CHAPTER THREE

Public Places and Mass Shootings

On May 14, 2022, Payton S. Gendron shot thirteen people at Tops Friendly Market in East Buffalo, New York. It was the worst shooting in Buffalo history—and a racially motivated hate crime. Of the thirteen people shot, eleven were Black and two were white. All ten of the victims killed were Black. The heavily armed white teenager fired fifty shots outside and inside the grocery store.

Tops Friendly Market stood right in the center of a disinvested Black community. The shooting hit the community in three ways. First, ten people were killed and three were injured while doing an everyday activity. No one expects a trip to the grocery store to be life-threatening.

Second, Tops Friendly Market was the only grocery store in that area. When it was shut down for a while after the shooting, the neighborhood didn't have access to food or a community place for gathering. Also, when the store was closed, there was no place for people in search of healing from the mass shooting to meet up other than churches. Communities affected by mass shootings need a place to heal, a place to come together to process their emotions and experiences and support one another. Having lost the only

Community members gathered near Tops Friendly Market to pray and mourn after the attack.

place to get food in the area, a community gathering place, and a place to come together for healing made the trauma of the mass shooting worse for the community.

Third, Gendron shot people because of white supremacist ideology. Gendron posted online that he chose Tops Friendly Market as his target because that area in Buffalo had a higher Black population than other locations he was considering. He also visited Tops Friendly Market many times to plan his attack, noting how many Black people visited the market.

Gendron pled guilty to fifteen counts, including murder in the first degree and attempted murder motivated by hate. He was sentenced to eleven life terms in prison. In 2023 he also faced federal hate crime charges, which could lead to the death penalty.

Mass shootings like the one at Tops Friendly Market have become commonplace in the US. In 2021 there were 686 mass shootings in the US, the highest amount ever recorded. In 2022, 600 people were killed and 2,700 wounded in mass shootings. In 2023 the US had more than one mass shooting per day, according to the Gun Violence Archive. And it's not just the US. In Mexico and Canada, mass shootings are becoming more common too. Mass shootings are also on the rise in Europe, though the numbers for other countries are nowhere near US rates.

> "I definitely know that she wouldn't want me to be consumed by sadness and anger. I will definitely try to find strength in her memory and use it to fight injustice and racism for the rest of my life in her name."
>
> —Mark Talley, son of Tops Friendly Market shooting victim Geraldine Talley

Gun Violence Archive

A nonprofit organization based in Washington, DC, runs the Gun Violence Archive. The archive catalogs information from more than 7,500 sources, including law enforcement, governmental, media, and commercial sources, to keep track of gun violence in the US in real time. Researchers, analysts, and journalists then use the data to discuss gun violence and educate others.

One of Canada's worst mass shootings happened in 2020 when a shooter killed twenty-two people in twelve hours in rural Nova Scotia. A memorial was set up at a former church in the town of Portapique where the mass shooting began.

Defining a Mass Shooting

What qualifies as a mass shooting depends on where it takes place and who labels it. For example, the Gun Violence Archive describes a mass shooting as an incident where four or more people are wounded or killed. These shootings, like many other incidents of gun violence, are between people who may know each other. Under this definition, cities including Los Angeles, Baltimore, Philadelphia, and Detroit had a significant percentage of the 656 mass shootings the organization recorded in 2023.

However, the New York–based Rockefeller Institute of Government has a slightly different definition of a mass shooting. In this definition, a mass shooting is an incident of targeted violence carried out by one or more people in a public location chosen either at random or for symbolic value. Mass shooters, according to the Rockefeller Institute, are mostly men (96 percent) and white (54 percent). They are 33.4 years old on average and primarily use handguns in their shootings (75 percent). But the use of semiautomatic weapons and long rifles in mass shootings has increased due to easier access. Most mass shootings happen in the workplace (31 percent) or at a store (17 percent).

Locations of Mass Shootings according to the National Institute of Justice 2018 Study

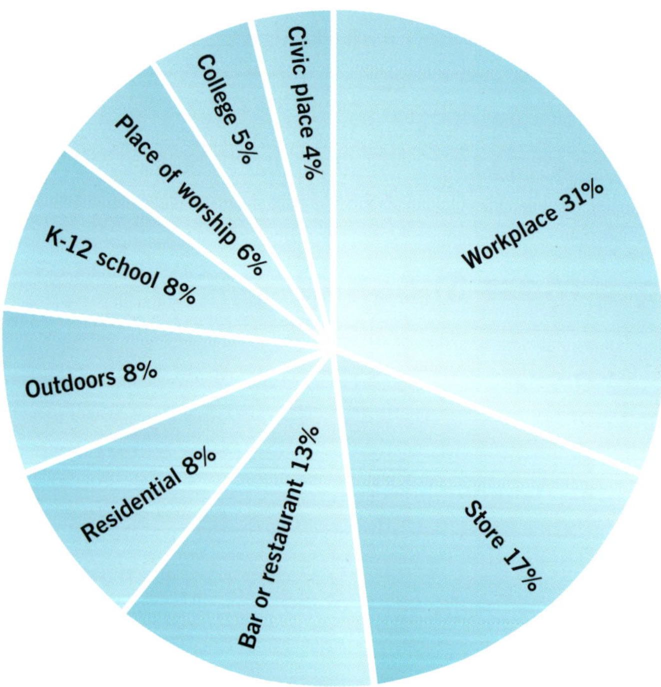

Source: National Institute of Justice, "Public Mass Shootings: Database Amasses Details of a Half Century of U.S. Mass Shootings with Firearms, Generating Psychosocial Histories," February 3, 2022, nij.ojp.gov:https://nij.ojp.gov/topics/articles/public-mass-shootings-database-amasses-details-half-century-us-mass-shootings.

Motivations for Mass Shootings

After a mass shooting, lawmakers and individuals often ask why. Why did the mass shooting happen? Why did it happen at a specific place? But focusing on just the specific whys doesn't always explain the big picture of why a mass shooter causes so much violence. Motivations for mass shootings vary. But some researchers think the various pathways to inflicting such gun violence are similar.

In 2018 the National Institute of Justice, the research arm of the US Department of Justice, partnered with the Violence Project, a research center at Hamline University in Minnesota that focuses on mass shootings and violence reduction. They put together a database that would bring some insight into why people commit mass shootings. They found that many mass shooters had experienced childhood trauma and been exposed to violence at a young age. Thirty-one percent of mass shooters had experienced some form of childhood trauma, and 80 percent of them were in a crisis related to that trauma at the time of the offense.

In 1949 Howard Unruh (*center*) killed thirteen people in Camden, New Jersey, with a pistol. Many historians consider this to be the US's first modern mass shooting. Many of the victims were people that he knew from his neighborhood.

About 70 percent of mass shooters were familiar with at least some of their victims. Almost half of the

Calling a Truce

Unlike mass shootings, most instances of gun violence start as arguments at their core. In-person arguments, disputes at school, and arguments beginning on social media sites such as Facebook, Instagram, and X (formerly Twitter) are just some examples of how gun violence starts. If someone gets upset enough and has access to a gun, these arguments can escalate quickly and spiral into instances of gun violence.

REFLECT
What are some alternatives to violence when people have disagreements or conflicts?

Reducing gun violence as a solution to solving arguments and using conflict resolution instead has been the mission of nonprofits nationwide, including Youth Restorative Services in Montgomery County, Maryland; Kids Managing Conflict in Sunset Beach, California; and Committee for Children in Seattle, Washington.

In Philadelphia there's even an app for conflict resolution. The Philly Truce app is a 24-7 service that brings together mediators and people in conflict to try and stop a shooting before it starts. Using the app, someone connected to the conflict reaches out, and volunteers respond. In addition to stopping conflicts, the Philly Truce app also connects its users to mental health counseling, food and shelter, and other services.

Alisi Finau (*front left*) and Michael Zamora (*front right*) practice conflict resolution at Charles M. Goethe Middle School in Sacramento, California. Developing conflict resolution skills could help reduce rates of gun violence.

Garnell Whitfield Jr.'s mother, Ruth, was killed in the Tops Friendly Market shooting. Whitfield urged the US government to act against white supremacy and gun violence at a Senate committee on domestic terrorism in 2022.

people who committed mass shootings had shared their plans with someone before they did it, usually a coworker, friend, or family member. Many of them also left manifestos, written statements declaring the motives behind the shooting.

In the mass shooting at Tops Friendly Market, Gendron fit many of these criteria. For example, he wanted to make sure that his manifesto was easily accessible, so he posted it on Google Docs. He also wore a GoPro camera because he wanted to broadcast the attack on Twitch, a social media application that allows content creators to broadcast live videos. A study of mass shootings between 2010 and 2019 found that 78 percent of mass shooters were motivated by needing attention.

Grievance

The Tops Friendly Market shooting also shows another part of what often drives mass shooters—a perception of grievance. Grievances are real or perceived problems that a person experiences. In Gendron's case, the grievance was the perceived lack of opportunity that he saw for himself as a white man. Gendron believed in the Great Replacement Theory. This unfounded idea suggests that non-white people and culture are replacing white people and culture. Although scholars and experts have disputed the theory, the prejudices connected to it have still impacted non-white communities.

Grievance also plays a part in many school and workplace mass shootings. The shooters are often people who have either worked in that workplace or who have attended the school—they have a connection to it. For example, in December 2023 Anthony Polito, a man who had applied to be a professor at the University of Nevada, Las Vegas, was turned down for the job. Once he found out that the school had rejected his application, he came into a campus building, killed three people, wounded a fourth, and was later killed in a shootout with police.

The community of Parkland, Florida, held a candlelight vigil to mourn the seventeen people killed in the 2018 school shooting at Marjory Stoneman Douglas High School. The shooter's grievance was that he was expelled from the school.

A memorial site for the victims of the Robb Elementary School shooting in Uvalde, Texas. Nineteen students and two teachers were killed on May 24, 2022. The shooter was a former student at the school.

School Shootings

Some consider the April 20, 1999, mass shooting at Columbine High School in Littleton, Colorado, to be the first major school shooting in the US. Two teenagers, Eric Harris and Dylan Klebold, killed twelve students and one teacher in less than twenty minutes. They also wounded twenty other students and one teacher during that time. The shooters used semiautomatic rifles, pistols, and explosives as students hid and ran for their lives.

Mass Shootings and Mass Media

Mass media is a collective term that describes broadcasting, the Internet, and print media such as newspapers, magazines, and books. The mass media coverage surrounding the Columbine school shooting was extensive and sensationalized, focusing on the shooters and their motives. Shooters often get a huge amount of attention in the media, and often that is exactly what mass shooters want. The shooters frequently get more attention in mass media than the victims.

Arapahoe County District Attorney Carol Chambers addresses the media following a hearing on a mass shooting in Aurora, Colorado, in 2012.

Some researchers say that how the media covers mass shootings inspires others to commit similar crimes. They call it the contagion effect. The contagion effect implies that one mass shooting leads to others in nearby areas.

"So one happens and you see another few happen right after that," says crime scientist Jillian Peterson, founder of the Violence Project. Researchers also found that there is a window of time lasting about two weeks when a mass shooting is most likely to lead to more mass shootings.

REFLECT

How is gun violence portrayed in the media? Do you think it is accurate? Why or why not?

Since Columbine, there had been more than 730 incidents of gun violence at schools as of 2023, accounting for hundreds of deaths and injuries among students, teachers, and others on school grounds. And school shootings keep happening. Behind the US, Mexico has the second highest global rate of school shootings. Canada is ranked ninth.

There has also been a recent increase in school shootings, with 2021, 2022, and 2023 all setting records since 2008. Only five states in the US (Montana, Wyoming, New Hampshire, Vermont, and Rhode Island) have not had any school shootings between the years of 2008 and 2023.

One of the most infamous school shootings took place in Newtown, Connecticut. It was one of the deadliest school shootings in US history. On December 14, 2012, Adam Lanza killed his mother with a gun that she had purchased

In 2018 high school students protested the US's lack of gun control laws by lying in front of the White House.

On the steps at the Capitol in Washington DC, US representative Lucy McBath speaks at a rally with the Gun Violence Prevention Task Force members in 2023. The event marked the eleventh anniversary of the Sandy Hook Elementary School shooting.

legally on his behalf. He then took that same gun and went to the elementary school he had attended as a child, Sandy Hook Elementary School, and killed twenty children and six adults before turning the gun on himself.

Like all mass shootings, school shootings are frightening, dangerous events. But some people and organizations are working to help keep people safe in the event of a school shooting. After the Sandy Hook shooting, community members of Newtown created a group called Sandy Hook Promise. Their mission is to protect children from gun violence. They have created training programs that have led to safer schools nationwide. Their Know the Signs program teaches youth and adults how to identify at-risk behaviors, and how to intervene and get help.

Schools are also using other means to help students stay safer. In many school districts, young people learn how to protect themselves in the event of a mass shooting. They practice active shooter drills designed to show them where to find safety if a mass shooting occurs. Students might also learn how to find an escape route, hide or seek shelter, or fight to stay alive.

School Resource Officers

While neither the Columbine nor Sandy Hook shootings led to major legislative changes, they did make communities think long and hard about ways to prevent them from happening again. The shootings helped increase public attention on school safety and gun violence. They also led police departments to train rapid-response police officers. And while police officers had been in schools since the 1950s, what happened at Columbine was one of the factors that led to an increased police presence in schools.

Some schools are using school safety dogs to help prevent gun violence. In 2019 Clark County School District K9 Officer James Harris and his partner Ziggy, a gun-sniffing labrador retriever, searched for a gun during a training session at Desert Pines High School in Las Vegas, Nevada.

More than twenty-three thousand sworn School Resource Officers (SROs) worked in schools at the end of the 2020 school year. SROs are police officers who use a community-based approach to address and reduce crime, violence, and disruptive behaviors in schools.

Because SROs are actual law enforcement officers, roughly 99 percent of them are armed with guns. Some trusting relationships have formed between students and SROs. While the SRO's job is to help schools be safer and to protect students from any dangers, students have also helped police solve crimes outside the school by giving them information.

It is not fully clear how effective SROs are. Two studies showed that having more SROs in school did not improve school safety. But another study found that having SROs in middle schools lowered serious violence. Regardless, not everyone agrees that SROs can keep schools safe. Some people feel less safe knowing that someone in the school building is armed.

***Left to right*: School Resource Officers Leon Leonard, Leonardo Carillo, and Claudia Beltrand from Miami-Dade County Public Schools in Miami, Florida, speak to students at Miami Jackson High School in 2017.**

Public Safety

Besides having SROs to maintain school safety, some schools also use metal detectors at entrances. Metal detectors are increasingly being used in both schools and public spaces to detect guns or other metal objects that could threaten people's safety. In public spaces such as airports, stadiums, and government buildings, metal detectors are commonly used to prevent individuals from carrying weapons in.

Bag size restrictions in public places have also become increasingly common for public safety. By limiting the size of bags allowed into public spaces, authorities hope to make it more difficult for individuals to conceal weapons in large bags. In addition to limiting the size of bags, some venues restrict the type of bags allowed. They may require transparent or mesh bags for easier visual inspection of the bags' contents. The National Football League and Major League Baseball often provide clear plastic totes at their stadiums for their fans to purchase and use to carry their belongings.

Bag restrictions and metal detectors can work to try and keep guns out of public places. But the Federal Emergency Management Agency says the best thing people can do to stay safe is to be prepared and respond effectively to emergencies. The agency suggests that people stay alert, say something if they see something, and have an exit plan wherever they go.

REFLECT

Do you have any ideas of other safety measures that could be taken in schools or public spaces? What are they?

CHAPTER FOUR

"I Used to Love Outside"

Saiyonn Thomas was an athlete and spent a lot of time outdoors. He liked hanging out with friends and playing basketball at the recreation center in his neighborhood. But in April 2023 everything changed. He was at the McDonald's in his Philadelphia neighborhood, grabbing a snack and hanging out with friends. As they shook hands in the parking lot and headed their separate ways, shots rang out, and a bullet hit him.

"I used to love [being] outside," he said. "I was playing football and I box, so outside was my thing. But I got shot and [post-traumatic stress disorder (PTSD)] kicked in. I don't know who shot me, so it's like, I've gotta watch everybody, even my closest homies. So now, nine times out of ten, if I'm not at work or with my son, I'm in the house."

REFLECT

What would you like to see done by the government or in your community for people impacted by gun violence like Saiyonn Thomas was?

Gun violence can hinder young people's health and well-being, leading to symptoms including anxiety, withdrawal, anger, depression, inability to sleep, constant fear, and inability to concentrate.

PTSD

According to the American Psychiatric Association, people with PTSD have intense, disturbing thoughts and feelings connected to an experienced trauma that last for a long time. They may also relive the trauma through flashbacks or nightmares and may want to keep to themselves as a result. PTSD impacts soldiers who have experienced combat, victims of abuse, and others who have experienced profound trauma. The disorder is also becoming more common among young people exposed to gun violence.

Many young people are exposed to gun violence, even if they are not directly injured. A 2024 study found that 8 percent of children and 13 percent of teens in the US were exposed to a shooting in their lifetime.

A joint study in 2021 from the University of Pennsylvania Hospital and the Children's Hospital of Philadelphia shows that the number of mental health–related emergency room visits by young people exposed to gun violence in the city's neighborhoods has increased, especially for people who live within five blocks of a shooting. The research focused on people between the ages of zero and nineteen from twelve Philadelphia zip codes. Researchers also looked at the number of emergency room visits from this group relating to PTSD, depression, using harmful substances such as drugs, and other mental health–related emergencies. They then cross-referenced the emergency room visits with Philadelphia Police

Department data to see how many of these people had been exposed to gun violence within sixty days before those emergency room visits.

"Gun violence affects the whole community, beyond the victims who are personally injured."
—Dr. Aditi Vasan, Children's Hospital of Philadelphia

Of the 54,341 young people studied, 43,143 of them had been exposed to gun violence within sixty days before a mental health emergency room visit. Young people living within two or three blocks of a shooting were more likely to visit the emergency room for a mental health–related emergency.

The Kaiser Family Foundation found similar results in a national study they conducted in 2024 that looked at the connection between young people and trauma. According to the study, the risk of mental health challenges, poor performance in school, and substance use increased if a person was a victim of gun violence. Understanding this data about the direct relationship between trauma and gun violence in young people can be used to help them get the support and services they need.

Gun violence disproportionately affects Black youth and families. In 2022 Black youth accounted for 48 percent of all youth firearm deaths, although they made up only 14 percent of the US population.

Working through It

Oronde McClain was waiting for a friend of his mother's at a bus stop. He wanted to help her carry her groceries. It took a while for the bus to arrive, so he decided to wait at a nearby Chinese takeout restaurant. As he was waiting, he was hit in the back of the head with a stray bullet. He was ten years old.

For years after, McClain struggled with partial paralysis, anxiety, and depression because of the shooting. He also has PTSD.

There is no one way to handle PTSD. "But you can control it with help," says McClain, who later wrote a book called *PTSD Won't Define Me*. People who develop PTSD have it for the rest of their lives. Memories of the trauma they suffered won't completely go away. However, there are ways to address it.

McClain stresses the importance of building a support network of friends and family who can understand and empathize. Connecting with others who are gun violence survivors and who are going through PTSD can be very helpful. "Every survivor's story is different but it is the same," McClain said.

Other ways to address PTSD include acknowledging difficult feelings and emotions. For victims of gun violence, feeling rage toward the shooter or experiencing guilt or shame for not doing more to help are common and normal reactions. Coping with PTSD is a journey that requires patience and persistence. Recovery doesn't happen overnight, but people can learn to manage their symptoms and lead fulfilling lives with time, effort, and the right support.

McClain is an activist who helps victims of gun violence. He hosts many events and organizes peaceful protests in Philadelphia.

CHAPTER FIVE

It's Up to Us

Many governments in North America are working to prevent and decrease gun violence. In 2020 when Canada saw that its gun violence rates had increased to a level unseen in the country since 1992, the government passed legislation banning assault weapons. Assault weapons are semiautomatic guns designed for military use and quick, efficient killing. Assault weapons are very lethal because of their rapid rate of fire. They are often the weapon of choice for mass shooters.

While Mexico already has strict gun laws, people smuggle thousands of guns into Mexico from the US every year. Because of that, in 2021 Mexico became the first country in the world to file a lawsuit against the gun industry in the US. US courts dismissed the case, but Mexico made an appeal and filed a second lawsuit against five gun dealers in Arizona. As of 2024 a trial date had yet to be set.

In 2022 Canada's government started a national handgun freeze. People living in Canada cannot buy, sell, or transfer handguns. They also cannot bring new handguns from another country into Canada. Lawmakers initiated the freeze

Perpetrators of the deadliest school shootings in the US, including that at Sandy Hook Elementary School, used assault weapons to commit their crimes. That's part of the reason people protest their availability for purchase and use.

because they found that handguns were the weapon of choice for most gun-related crimes.

In June 2022 the US Congress passed the Bipartisan Safer Communities Act. Under this law, people between the ages of eighteen and twenty-one wishing to buy a gun have to undergo a tighter background check that includes a search for juvenile criminal records. This act also defines who must register as a federally licensed gun dealer. The act targets other areas of gun control too. It turns gun trafficking into a federal offense. And it even goes further to make straw purchasing, which is buying a gun for someone who can't buy one legally, a federal offense too.

The Bipartisan Safer Communities Act also invests in mental health services for young people and families who are victims of gun violence. Congress provided funding in the act for grants. These grants help communities fund and support suicide prevention services, crisis response services, de-escalation training, and trauma-informed therapy.

In September 2023 US president Joe Biden established the Office of Gun Violence Prevention. Vice president Kamala Harris and Stefanie Feldman, a longtime adviser to Biden on gun policy, oversee the office. The office has advocated for laws requiring gun dealers to obtain federal gun licenses and conduct background checks before selling firearms.

US State Legislation to Stop Gun Violence

Several US states have also passed laws addressing gun control and gun violence prevention. In 2022 Delaware passed a bill to prohibit assault weapons. Also in 2022 the states of Washington, Delaware, and Rhode Island banned high-capacity magazines. A high-capacity magazine attaches to an assault weapon to allow many gunshots without needing to reload. It can hold more than ten to fifteen rounds of ammunition. When assault weapons or high-capacity magazines are used in mass shootings, 155 percent more people are shot, and 47 percent more people are killed.

In 2024 Michigan and Minnesota created red flag laws. These laws allow judges to temporarily remove guns from someone who is considered a threat to themselves or others. And in 2024 Washington state expanded background checks and created a waiting period before someone could buy a gun.

In 2022 US Representative Robin Kelly (*front right*) spoke during a rally at the US Capitol before the vote on the Bipartisan Safer Communities Act. The bill passed by a vote of 234–193. Biden signed the act into law on June 25, 2022.

Community Organization Work on Gun Violence

Community organizations are also trying to reduce and prevent gun violence. Chicago Survivors provides crisis response and support services to families and individuals affected by gun violence in Chicago, Illinois. Some of the services Chicago Survivors include are in-home family support counseling, youth trauma informed therapy, and survivor support groups.

Youth ALIVE in Oakland, California, works to prevent gun violence with their frontline staff who grew up in the communities that they serve. Their primary goals are to interrupt the cycle of violence on the streets of Oakland, convince angry victims and their loved ones not to retaliate, and provide ongoing support to the wounded and grieving. They have workshops and events including one held in 2023 entitled, "Healing Gun Violence in Latinx Communities."

The New Yorkers Against Gun Violence organization works with lawmakers, advocates, and survivors of gun violence. They lead rallies, marches, and protests to raise awareness of gun violence issues and advocate for gun reforms. Besides lobbying for support for laws addressing gun violence, they also educate New Yorkers about gun violence through community forums and workshops.

The Brady: United Against Gun Violence organization has made it their mission to reduce gun violence 25 percent in the US by 2025. The organization advocates for legislation and programs designed to end gun violence. They are actively working with members of the US Congress to push for the passage of laws aimed at preventing gun violence including universal background checks and banning assault weapons.

The Giffords Law Center works to research, enact, and defend proven laws and programs to reduce gun violence and save lives. Gabby Giffords, an Arizona congresswoman who was shot in the head during a mass shooting in 2011, cofounded the center.

The group PolySeSouvient advocates for stricter gun control laws in Canada. Following the mass shooting at Montreal's École Polytechnique University in 1989 that killed fourteen women, students at the school launched a petition for better gun control. Supported by more than 500 thousand signatures, the students work to pass legislation including

Aalayah Eastmond (*left*) prepares for an event with Robert Schentrup at Brady: United Against Gun Violence in Washington, DC, in 2018. Eastmond survived the mass shooting at Marjory Stoneman Douglas High School. Schentrup's sister Carmen was killed.

possession permits and the registration of all firearms in Canada. Students, graduates of the university, and families of the victims advocate for stricter gun licensing, stronger background checks, and further bans on assault weapons. Another group that works to reduce gun violence in Canada is the Coalition for Gun Control. This organization works toward stronger gun control measures and has been active in Canada for more than three decades.

The Reality Check

Before joining the Philadelphia City Council, Kenyatta Johnson started an organization called Peace Not Guns. He founded the organization after his cousin and several close childhood friends were murdered by gun violence. The idea behind the organization was to combat gun violence through educational programs and mentoring. Peace Not Guns also teaches young adults conflict resolution and anger management. Johnson's mission has become to create a city of peace, not guns.

Johnson held a Peace Not Guns roundtable discussion with teenagers at Philadelphia City Hall in 2023. He wanted to hear how gun violence impacts youth and what solutions they might have to keep people in the community safe. More than one hundred people attended. Johnson learned that you must be real in talking with youth about gun violence.

"I try, to the best of my ability to be real with them because this is reality, which is so unfortunate," Johnson said. "You have to be real with children around the issue of gun violence. They're growing up in the inner city. So, there's no way around being exposed."

In 2024 Johnson was elected Philadelphia City Council president and chair of the city council's Special Committee on Gun Violence Prevention. He has worked tirelessly to get Philadelphia to invest millions of dollars per year in community-based organizations to reduce gun violence.

Johnson is continuing to call for the city of Philadelphia to invest more money in trauma-informed therapy, especially for youth, and to address gun violence as a public health issue.

What Can Young People Do to Help Stop Gun Violence?

Many young people have been helping to call attention to gun violence and advocate for its prevention and reduction. They often work through groups they created themselves or with organizations that have worked with young people for a long time.

One of the more well-known organizations for young people fighting gun violence is March for Our Lives. A group of students created the organization after a mass shooting occurred at their school, Marjory Stoneman Douglas High School, in Parkland in February 2018. March for Our Lives has mobilized young people from around the US to not only take to the streets to protest and demand action from politicians to reduce gun violence in the US, but also to go to the voting booth and make their voices heard that way as well. March for Our Lives has helped pass more than three hundred gun safety laws across the United States.

Kenyatta Johnson (*right*) at a city council meeting in 2016. In 2021 he described the gun violence problem in Philadelphia as a moral, economic, racial, and human crisis.

March for Our Lives has also organized school walkouts. These walkouts involve students leaving their classrooms and schools for a period of time to protest gun violence and advocate for gun control legislation. The walkouts serve as a form of peaceful protest and a way for students to voice their concerns about gun violence in schools and communities across the US. It is important that young people get and stay involved. Your voice matters.

And while it is important to keep an eye on what's going on throughout North America, you're more directly impacted by the people who are in your local and municipal governments. Here are some things you can do in your community:

- Research and learn about local and state gun laws.
- Join or start a community group focused on addressing gun violence.
- Attend city council meetings to stay informed about policies and decisions related to gun violence prevention and community safety.
- Volunteer with local organizations.

Youth gathered at the March for Our Lives rally in San Francisco to call for gun control and end gun violence in 2018.

CONCLUSION
What Happens Now?

Whether gun violence gets worse will depend on what communities and governments do. If society continues to disinvest in urban communities where gun violence is most prevalent, it will get worse. If society doesn't realize that the use of guns to solve arguments doesn't work, it will get worse. If governments don't create better mental health services, it will get worse. And if people don't hold their governments accountable for allowing these things to continue and demand better for everyone, it will get worse.

But there is hope too. Many organizations, activists, and lawmakers are working to make a difference and help end gun violence. But most importantly, young people continue to be at the forefront of speaking up about gun violence. No matter where they stand on gun control, it is hoped that they will continue to feel empowered and speak up for themselves and their communities.

REFLECT

What do you think you could do to help make sure that you and your community are safe from gun violence?

GLOSSARY

activist: someone who actively campaigns for social or political change, often by participating in protests, demonstrations, or other forms of direct action

advocate: to support or argue for a cause or policy. An advocate is one who supports or promotes the interests of a cause or group.

background check: a process conducted by a government authority or licensed gun dealer to verify if a person can lawfully buy or possess a gun. It involves accessing databases to check for criminal history, mental health issues, or other factors that may disqualify the individual from owning a gun.

civilian: a person who is not on active duty in the armed forces or not on a police force

colonization: when a country establishes control over a group of people or an area outside its borders

conflict resolution: a method of peacefully settling arguments or disagreements by finding common ground and reaching agreements that satisfy all parties involved. It involves identifying the underlying issues, facilitating communication, and negotiating to prevent future tensions.

Democratic primary: a part of the election process where registered members of the Democratic party vote to choose their preferred candidate for a political office

discrimination: a prejudiced or biased outlook, action, or treatment

domestic violence: when one person hurts, kills, or controls another person in their family or household

gun permit: a license issued by a government authority granting permission to use a gun

homicide: the act of one person unlawfully causing the death of another person

ideology: a way of thinking of an individual or a group

inflict: to cause something unpleasant to be endured, such as harm, damage, or suffering

infringe: to violate a rule, law, right, or boundary

legislation: a formal process of proposing, debating, and passing laws that govern how people behave and interact in society. A legislator is someone who makes laws.

lobby: to influence lawmakers to create certain laws or policies that benefit an individual's or group's interests

manifesto: a written statement publicly declaring the motives, intentions, or views of the writer

marginalized: a social or economic process where individuals or groups are pushed to the edges or margins of society and excluded from the mainstream

marksmanship: the skill and ability to shoot accurately with guns, involving precise aim, control, and consistency in hitting targets

militia: a group of people organized for military purposes but who are not in the armed forces

perception: the brain's process of using information from the senses to create a mental picture or understanding of the world

personal freedom: an individual's ability to make choices and pursue their own interests, beliefs, and goals without interference from government, society, or other individuals

regulation: a rule dealing with details or procedure

segregation: the enforced separation of individuals or groups based on certain characteristics such as race, ethnicity, religion, or gender

silencer: a device attached to the muzzle of a gun to reduce the noise and muzzle flash when the gun is fired

structural inequality: differences in opportunities that are built into the social, economic, and political systems of a society. Some people have more disadvantages than others because of factors such as their race, gender, or how much money they have.

trauma: a term used to describe deeply distressing or harmful experiences that can have lasting effects on a person's mental or emotional well-being

trauma-informed therapy: an approach to counseling that considers a person's past traumatic experiences

SOURCE NOTES

10 "A well-regulated Militia . . . shall not be infringed.": "Amdt2.2 Historical Background on Second Amendment. Constitution Annotated, Analysis and Interpretation of the US Constitution," accessed February 10, 2024, https://constitution.congress.gov/browse/essay/amdt2-2/ALDE_00013262/.

22–23 "YouthBuild sits . . . of gun violence.": Le'Yondo Dunn, "Interview with Le'Yondo Dunn," interview by Denise Clay-Murray, August 31, 2023.

26 "I definitely know . . . in her name.": Carolyn Thompson, "Victims of Buffalo Supermarket Mass Shooting Remembered 1 Year After Racist Massacre," PBS News Hour, May 14, 2023, https://www.pbs.org/newshour/nation/victims-of-buffalo-supermarket-mass-shooting-remembered-1-year-after-racist-massacre.

34 "So one happens . . . right after that.": Rhitu Chatterjee, "Mass Shootings Can Be Contagious, Research Shows," National Public Radio, January 24, 2023, https://www.npr.org/sections/health-shots/2019/08/06/748767807/mass-shootings-can-be-contagious-research-shows.

40 "I used to . . . in the house.": Saiyonn Thomas, "Interview with Saiyonn Thomas," interview by Denise Clay-Murray, November 6, 2023.

43 "Gun violence affects . . . are personally injured.": "Gun Violence Exposure Associated with Higher Rates of Mental Health-Related ED Visits by Children," Penn Medicine News, September 20, 2021, https://www.pennmedicine.org/news/news-releases/2021/september/gun-violence-exposure-associated-with-higher-rates-of-mental-health-related-ed-visits-by-children.

44 "But you can . . . it with help.": A Survivor on Why it Takes a Village (and Forgiveness) to End Gun Violence," Red Blue & Brady Podcast, Brady United, September 9, 2022, https://www.bradyunited.org/podcast/episodes/oronde-mcclain-gun-violence-survivor-forgiveness-healing.

44 "Every survivor's story. . . is the same.": Ibid.

52 "I try, to . . . around being exposed.": Kenyatta Johnson, "An Interview with Councilmember Kenyatta Johnson," interview by Denise Clay-Murray, December 12, 2023.

SELECTED BIBLIOGRAPHY

Adams, Destinee. "Is Gun Violence an Epidemic in the US? Experts and History Say It Is." National Public Radio, June 29, 2023. https://www.npr.org/2023/06/29/1184731316/gun-violence-epidemic-suicide-mass-shooting-public-health-emergency-chicago.

"The Facts that Make Us Act." Brady Center to Prevent Gun Violence. Accessed May 25, 2024. https://www.bradyunited.org/key-statistics.

"Gun Violence Survivors in America." Everytown For Gun Safety, February 27, 2023. https://everytownresearch.org/report/gun-violence-survivors-america/.

"It Ends with Us." March For Our Lives, August 2021. https://marchforourlives.com/wp-content/uploads/2021/08/It-Ends-With-Us-March-For-Our-Lives.pdf.

"100 Shooting Review Committee Report." City of Philadelphia, Committee on Public Safety and Special Committee on Gun Violence. Accessed February 9, 2024. https://phlcouncil.com/wp-content/uploads/2022/01/100-Shooting-Review-complete.pdf.

"The Root Causes of Gun Violence." The Educational Fund to Stop Gun Violence, March 2020. https://efsgv.org/wp-content/uploads/2020/03/EFSGV-The-Root-Causes-of-Gun-Violence-March-2020.pdf.

Schaeffer, Katherine. "Key Facts about Americans and Guns." Pew Research Center, September 13, 2023. https://www.pewresearch.org/short-reads/2023/09/13/key-facts-about-americans-and-guns/.

Schildkraut, Jaclyn, and H. Jaymi Elsass. "Mass Shooting Fact Sheet." The Rockefeller Institute of Government. Accessed May 15, 2024. https://rockinst.org/gun-violence/mass-shooting-factsheet/.

Towers, S., A. Gomez-Liveane, M. Khan, A. Mubayi, and C. Castillo-Chavez. "Contagion in Mass Killings and School Shootings." PLOS ONE, July 2, 2015. https://doi.org/10.1371/journal.pone.0117259.

FURTHER INFORMATION

Books

Bajramovic, Hana. *Whose Right Is It? The Second Amendment and the Fight over Guns*. New York: Henry Holt and Company, 2020.
This book examines the Second Amendment, looking at the history and stories behind the right to bear arms.

Doeden, Matt. *Gun Violence: Fighting for Our Lives and Our Rights*. Minneapolis: Twenty-First Century Books, 2020.
This book explores gun violence, gun control, the history of guns and gun laws in the United States, and the devastation of mass shootings.

Jewell, Tiffany, and Aurelia Durand. *This Book Is Anti-Racist: 20 Lessons on How to Wake Up, Take Action, and Do The Work*. London: Frances Lincoln Children's Books, 2020.
This interactive workbook invites teens to explore and understand racism. It includes activities, reflections, and lessons to inspire young readers to become actively anti-racist.

McClain, Oronde. *PTSD Won't Define Me*. Philadelphia: McClain and Schaeffer Group, 2021.
This book dives into the struggle of having post-traumatic stress disorder after experiencing gun violence.

Reynolds, Jason, and Ibram X. Kendi. *Stamped: Racism, Antiracism, and You: A Remix of the National Book Award-winning Stamped from the Beginning*. New York: Little, Brown Books for Young Readers, 2020.
This adaptation of Ibram X. Kendi's *Stamped from the Beginning* provides an accessible and engaging history of racism in America. Jason Reynolds delivers a compelling narrative that encourages critical thinking about the impact of racism on society.

Smith, Nareissa. *Fighting for Equality: Racial Justice in North America*. Minneapolis: Twenty-First Century Books, 2025.
With a focus on reflection, this book not only educates readers about the historical and contemporary challenges faced by marginalized racial groups in North America but also empowers them to become agents of change in the ongoing fight for racial justice.

Websites

Amnesty International

https://www.amnesty.org/en/what-we-do/arms-control/gun-violence/

This website provides definitions and statistics pertaining to the connection between discrimination and gun violence.

Brady: United Against Gun Violence

https://www.bradyunited.org

This group is dedicated to preventing gun violence, and its site provides resources on how communities can join to end gun violence. This site has statistics on how many people are shot in the US, how many people are injured by gunshots, and the daily gun violence numbers impacting people in the US. It also explains the relationship between disinvestment and gun violence.

Everytown for Gun Safety

https://everytown.org

Everytown for Gun Safety is a movement working to end gun violence. This website includes research, news, and resources related to gun safety.

Giffords Law Center

https://giffords.org/

The Giffords Law Center creates and advocates for gun safety laws. Their website also provides information on gun violence prevention.

National Institute of Justice-Gun Violence Research

https://nij.ojp.gov/topics/crime/violent-crime/gun-violence

The National Institute of Justice is the research and evaluation agency of the US Department of Justice. This website provides research and resources on criminal justice topics, including gun violence.

The Trace

https://www.thetrace.org/

This site explores the role of the gun industry in US gun violence. It also has a questions section where the reader can ask a question about guns or gun violence and other readers can answer. This site dives into the people, policies, and programs that are working to prevent gun violence.

INDEX

ABOUT THE AUTHOR

Denise Clay-Murray is a writer from Wilmington, Delaware. This is her first book for young readers. Her areas of expertise include politics, social justice, the arts, and food. When she isn't writing, she enjoys going to the movies, going to baseball games, and baking for her friends and family.

PHOTO ACKNOWLEDGMENTS

The images in this book are used with the permission of: © Jim West/Alamy Photo, p. 5; © Nick Wagner/AP Images, p. 6; © Gregory Bull/AP Images, p. 7; © Daniel Dempster Photography/Alamy Photo, p. 8; © Sheila Fitzgerald/Shutterstock Images, p. 9; © Library of Congress, p. 11; © Harry Thomas Flower/Shutterstock Images, p. 12; © Terri Laurens/Shutterstock Images, p. 13; © Brian N Rogers/Shutterstock Images, p. 14; © Thomas R Machnitzki/Wikimedia Commons, p. 16; © SNEHIT PHOTO/Adobe Stock, p. 17; © National Archives and Records Administration, p. 19; © Eric O. Ledermann/Shutterstock Images, p. 21; © SABINA PIERCE/AP Images, p. 23; © UPI/Alamy Photo, pp. 25, 34; © Pete Stevens/Shutterstock Images, p. 27; © AP Images, p. 29; © ZUMA Press, Inc./Alamy Photo, p. 30; © dpa picture alliance/Alamy Photo, pp. 31, 49; © SOPA Images Limited/Alamy Photo, p. 32; © US Department of Homeland Security/Wikimedia Commons, p. 33; © Joseph Gruber/Shutterstock Images, p. 35; © Imago/Alamy Photo, p. 36; © STEVE MARCUS/AP Images, p. 37; © Tribune Content Agency LLC/Alamy Photo, pp. 38, 51; © motortion/Adobe Stock, p. 41; © SpeedKingz/Shutterstock Images, p. 42; © DC Studio/Adobe Stock, p. 43; © ANGELA WEISS/Getty Images, p. 45; © JP Photography/Adobe Stock, p. 47; © Philadelphia City Council/Wikimedia Commons, p. 53; © Shelly Rivoli/Alamy Photo, p. 54.

Cover Photo: © Jacob Lund/Shutterstock Images

Design Elements: © Ezhevika/Shutterstock Images